ALL THE COLORS OF ME

PICTURING MY RESILIENCE

KNOWING AND SHOWING MY FEELINGS THROUGH ART

ANNA SHEPHERD
illustrated by ALICIA MÁS

PowerKiDS press.

Published in 2027
by The Rosen Publishing Group, Inc.
2544 Clinton Street, Buffalo, NY 14224

First published in Great Britain in 2023 by Hodder & Stoughton

Credits

Series Editor: Grace Glendinning

Series Designer: Alicia Más

Illustrations: Alicia Más

Cataloging-in-Publication Data

Names: Shepherd, Anna, author. | Más, Alicia, illustrator.
Title: Picturing my resilience / Anna Shepherd, illustrated by Alicia Más.
Description: Buffalo, New York : PowerKids Press, 2027. | Series: All the colors of me
Identifiers: ISBN 9781499458824 (pbk.) | ISBN 9781499458831 (library bound) | ISBN 9781499458848 (ebook)
Subjects: LCSH: Resilience (Personality trait) in children--Juvenile literature. | Self-actualization (Psychology)--Juvenile literature. | Self-confidence in children--Juvenile literature.
Classification: LCC BF723.R46 S547 2027 | DDC 155.41824--dc23

Printed in China

CPSIA Compliance Information: Batch #QS27PK. For further information contact Rosen Publishing at 1-800-237-9932.

CONTENTS

LISTENING TO OUR FEELINGS

We all have lots of feelings! They come and go – sometimes quickly, sometimes slowly.

Resilience is something we use for bouncing back after a tricky time, such as **losing** a pet, **changing** schools, or a **big argument** with a friend.

Life isn't always easy, but the keys to resilience are **trying hard**, **not giving up,** and **moving on** from disappointment!

DID YOU KNOW THAT YOU CAN GROW YOUR RESILIENCE BY PUSHING YOURSELF JUST THE RIGHT AMOUNT?

Can you think of something that you managed to do even though it seemed like a really big challenge at first?

Can you imagine if you had just said, "I give up. It's too hard!"

You didn't, though, which shows that you are already experienced with resilience!

ART-MAKING CAN HELP

Art-making can be a great way to notice and practice your resilience.

Art can help you to put feelings down on paper and express yourself – **with or without words!**

If we can get our feelings out and make sense of them with someone we trust, it can help us to move on.

Sometimes simply doing art can make us feel a bit better if we are having a tough time.

PLAY, HAVE FUN, and ENJOY being CREATIVE.

We can also use art as a helpful reminder of times when we have succeeded.

Remember when you were scared about something, but you did it anyway and it went better than expected?

Why not make a picture to celebrate that moment?

How can you show how that bravery felt?

You might think, "But I'm no good at art!" (Impossible!) But you don't have to worry about what it will look like. It is all about DOING. Then we see how the DOING helps us understand our feelings.

So let's get creative and see what happens!

You can always **KEEP** your **BRAVERY** artwork and look at it the next time you need to find your courage.

Making art can help us learn more about what

RESILIENCE IS.

Have you ever felt like you made a mistake or failed?

It might not feel nice to think about it.
You might feel embarrassed or ashamed.

Start your art! On a big piece of paper, can you show those tricky feelings in colors, shapes, or pictures?

Now add a layer to your art to show what helped you move on at the time.

* Was it words of encouragement?
* Was there an exciting goal you were determined to achieve?
* What kept you going?

Next add some new textures, colors, or shapes over and around your picture to show those feelings of determination and encouragement.

How would that look on the page?

Have a look at your picture now – has it helped you **feel differently about** that memory?

It helps to look at the FULL picture of a time when you **learned from**, **moved on,** and **grew** after a mistake.

THIS IS RESILIENCE!

Mistakes are a great way to learn about and grow resilience.

Next, we use our creativity to think about what

RESILIENCE FEELS LIKE.

Let's imagine it from the inside out ...

Here is a diagram of how to make an origami box. It is a bit tricky so it might take a few attempts.

Start by noticing what you are feeling in your body when one of the steps feels hard.

Do you feel frustrated and want to give up? Where do you feel that **in your body?**

Try smiling and see how that feels in your body on top of the frustration.

What about if you have a big stretch or dance around the room? How do you feel inside now?

Finish off your origami and see if you feel any different.

Spotting frustration in your body and moving past that feeling helps your **grit** grow. Grit is your determination to not give up.

You could even decorate your origami box with your new skill as a reminder:

Sometimes it's hard to believe we can achieve something.
This is where your imagination comes in handy, to think about what

RESILIENCE LOOKS LIKE.

Imagine staring at a huge wall. On the other side of it is something that you really, really want.

You are going to need lots of grit and determination to find a way over it, especially at times when you are tired and want to give up.

Stand in front of a mirror and imagine you feel really small. You are saying to yourself that there is no way you can get over the wall.

Notice how your body looks and feels.

Now picture yourself as somebody who **can** get over the wall. What changes do you notice in your face and body? What thoughts fill your head?

Get some paper and draw a Resilient Me self-portrait.

Which YOU is going to reach your goal?

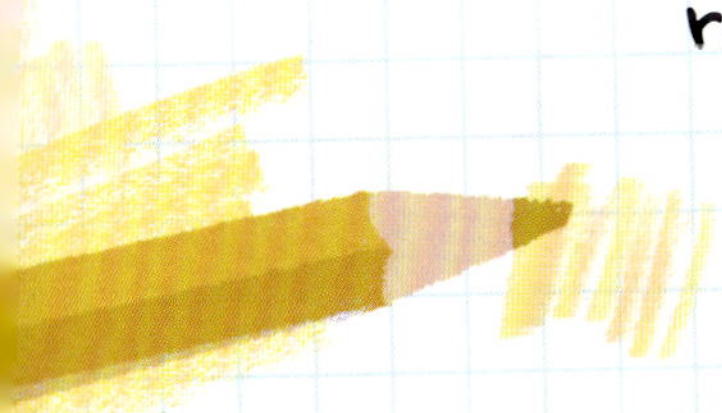

Next time you face a challenge, look at your Resilient Me picture. Remember how it looks and feels to believe you can do something.

You can use your creative mind to look ahead and consider what

RESILIENCE ACTS LIKE

in lots of different situations.

Now we jump ahead to the future!

Can you think of something in your future that might need some resilience?

For example, if you have a performance coming up or want to ask someone to play and are feeling shy, it can be helpful to **practice** these tricky things first. Try this with friends or family in a familiar place.

With a friend, you could also **act out** how you would **like** things to turn out. Drama is art, too!

Try being a character who is finding resilience tough. What could your friend say to encourage you?

You could also interview some adults in your life about times when they were resilient. Pretend you are a reporter and create a resilience newspaper to tell their story.

- How do you cope when you are not sure what is going to happen next? What is helpful?
- Do you like challenges?
- Is it OK to make mistakes?
- How do you feel when you try out something new?
- Do you finish things you start? If not, what stops you?
- How do you feel and act when you are disappointed? What helps you?
- Can you bounce back when you have felt upset about something? What helps?

Let's get familiar with some different

SHADES OF RESILIENCE.

The steps leading where you want to go aren't always direct! You might need different types of resilience along the way. You might **go up and down** some of the steps a few times before you succeed.

Picturing a Resilience Staircase can be very helpful.

The next time you have to do something that feels a bit difficult, look at the staircase and think about where you are on the steps.

Along the way, you might want to give your resilience a bit of a boost, using some of the skills in this book!

Notice which kinds of resilient behavior help you to move forwards.

SPEAKING OF RESILIENCE

is another way of growing your skills and changing your brain!

What we say to ourselves can really affect our actions and feelings.

I CAN'T

IT'S TOO HARD

I'LL GET IT WRONG

EVERYONE ELSE CAN DO THIS

I COULD GET HURT

I AM TRYING MY BEST

IT'S OK, I AM STILL LEARNING

I CAN'T DO IT YET

I AM LEARNING FROM MY MISTAKES

I AM CONFIDENT

I BELIEVE IN MYSELF

I AM BRAVE

Why not get creative and design a **positive phrases poster** to read in a strong voice each morning to remind yourself?

Which colors make you feel hopeful and powerful? Can you use those to decorate your words?

Your resilience is your own.
Try not to compare yourself to others.
Everyone has different challenges and
things that they find easier.

Can you take your poster even further to celebrate the unique person you are?

Draw or describe all the wonderful ways you are you:

Learning about our feelings is not a race!
All we need to aim for is:

SLOW AND STEADY RESILIENCE

Sticking with a challenge is part of resilience, but so is knowing when to ask for help or when to take a break.

You might not succeed **at all** at some things!

Resilience is also about dealing with disappointment.

As you deal with disappointments, it helps to surround yourself with things that **lift you up.**

Ask a friend to trace your body on a big piece of cardboard. Write or draw things that make you feel happy inside your life-sized picture.

Display or save your picture to remind you of those happy thoughts.

EVERYONE'S LIFE HAS UPS AND DOWNS.

Don't be afraid to take some time to recover and take care of your disappointment before you **try again**, **create a new plan,** or **move on.**

PRACTICING RESILIENCE

is fun to do when you're well rested and feeling ready to try.

Use this page in one of those moments so that when you really need it, you will be a resilience master.

Have a go at playing the Look on the Bright Side game.

With friends or family, each write out a pair of disappointments and bright sides. Mix them all up in a hat and work together to match them up as quickly as you can!

DISAPPOINTMENTS	BRIGHT SIDES
IT'S RAINING AND I CAN'T PLAY SOFTBALL, BUT ...	I CAN JUMP IN PUDDLES.
I DIDN'T GET PICKED FOR THE TEAM, BUT ...	NOW I HAVE MORE TIME TO PLAY WITH MY BROTHER.
I SPILLED MY MILK, BUT ...	AT LEAST THE GLASS DIDN'T BREAK!

You can also gather up good times to keep as evidence of your amazing resilience!

Start collecting happy memories of times you succeeded and times when you were kind to others and others were kind to you.

You can look at your Good Times Book whenever you feel doubtful or defeated.

Remember: if you are not feeling resilient one day, that's OK! You can grow your resilience for the next time by practicing and looking back at the art you've created in this book.

YOU ARE A RESILIENCE ARTIST!

Now that you've read this book, you are an expert resilience artist!

Here are even more fun ideas to keep your creativity and resilience flowing:

Decorate small, smooth pebbles. Keep them in your pocket and hold them when you need a bit of support.

Create a computer avatar of RESILIENT YOU! Give yourself a character name.

Think about designing a computer game where your character has to overcome challenges.

What is the goal and how will you achieve it? What will give you a boost or make it difficult? Will there be other characters that can help you?

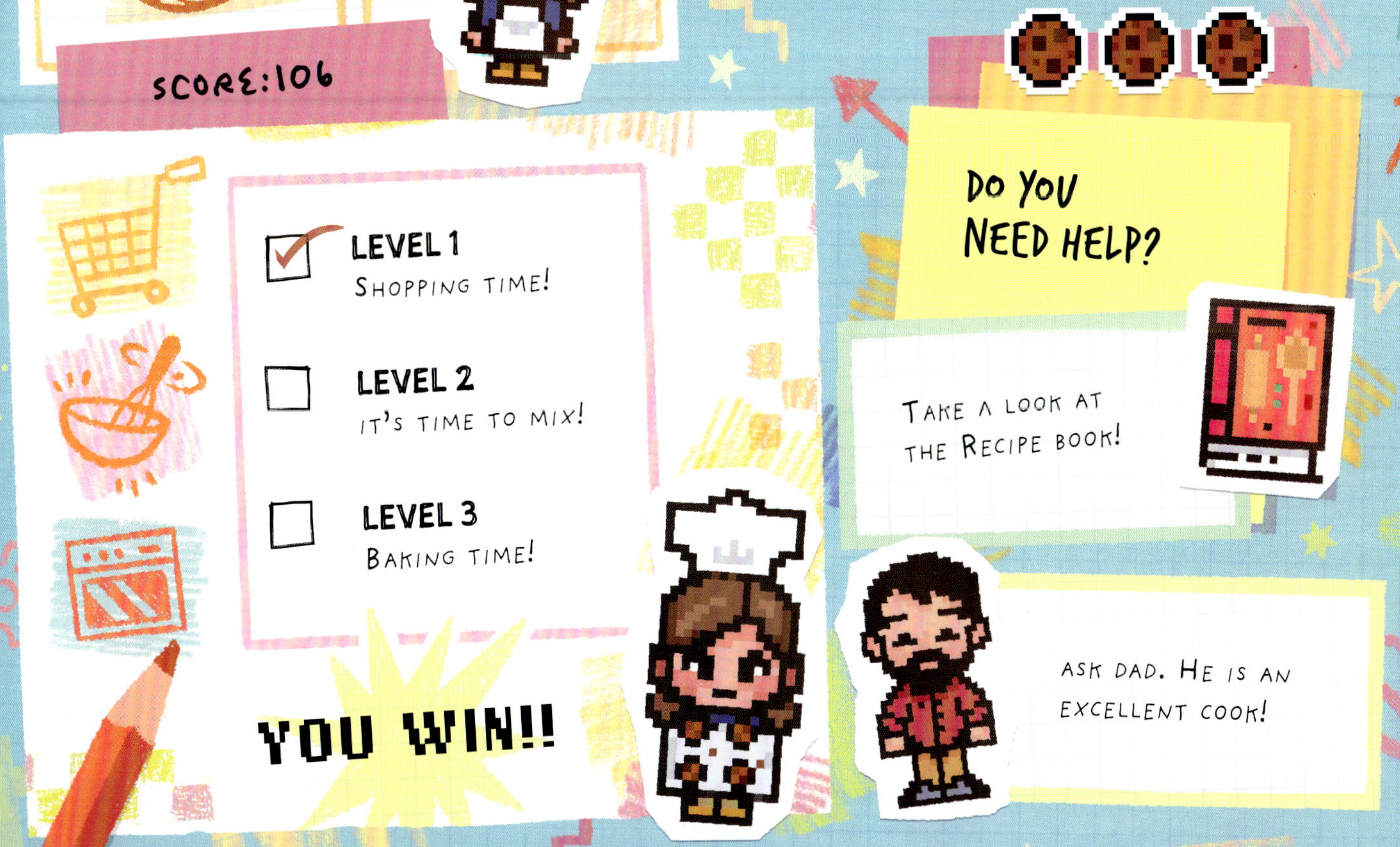

Think of something you really want to draw: a person, an animal, or your favorite superhero. You can look at art books or tutorials to learn how.

Draw a picture of this thing every day for two weeks. At the end of this time, look at your first picture and your last one. What do you notice? Which one is your favorite version?

Is there something creative you want to try but haven't, such as clay sculpting or painting with watercolors? What do you want to achieve and what are the steps to get there?

- [x] LOOK FOR BOOKS IN THE LIBRARY
- [x] TRY OUT A CLASS?
- [ ] ASK FRED ABOUT HIS ART
- [ ] ASK TO BORROW SOME MATERIALS
- [ ] TRY IT OUT!

Write out your answers and start ticking them off one by one. Don't forget to ask for help from a teacher or parent if needed. This is an important skill!

What new experiences do you want to have across your whole life? Why not make a vision board of all the things you want to try?

KEY TERMS

Avatar: a picture (moving or still) that stands in for you in a game or other activity.

Bravery: showing strength to face a fear or difficulty.

Challenging: describes something you find tricky.

Determination: the ability to continue trying to do something even if it is difficult.

Frustration: the feeling of being upset or annoyed by something, for example something you can't do.

Grit: the ability to stick at something.

Origami: a form of art that began in Japan, where you create something by folding paper.

Resilience: the ability to recover and learn from difficulties.

Sculpting: making 3-D art (not flat).

Texture: the feel or look of the surface of something.

Tutorial: when someone teaches others a certain skill.

BOOKS TO READ

***Kids Can Cope* series, by Gill Hasson (Franklin Watts)**

- *Bounce Back from Disappointment*
- *Face Your Fears*
- *Let Go of Jealousy*
- *Put Your Worries Away*
- *Say Hi When You're Shy*
- *Step Back from Frustration*
- *Take Charge of Anger*
- *Turn Away from Teasing*

***A World Full of Feelings* series, by Louise Spilsbury (Franklin Watts)**

- *Finding Calm*
- *Finding Courage*
- *Finding Happiness*
- *Finding Kindness*

***Build Resilience* series, by Honor Head (Franklin Watts)**

- *Anxiety and Self-Esteem*
- *Coping with Change*
- *Friendships and Bullying*
- *Unexpected Challenges*

WEBSITES to **VISIT** with the help of an adult:

Headspace.com

A website and app offering meditation and mindfulness tools to expand on the practice of understanding and dealing with emotions.

Youthmindfulness.org

Resources for mindfulness programs for young people.

HOW TO USE THIS BOOK: A GUIDE FOR ADULTS

This series of art therapy books has been developed to provide a creative starting point for further discussion and exploration around children's emotions.

Each book is intended for children to **share** with trusted adults, whether one-on-one or in a group setting in the classroom or elsewhere.

This book, *Picturing My Resilience*, is a careful exploration of the look and feel of all kinds of resilience. When dealing with any emotion, big or small, the utmost priority is making children feel **safe and heard** as they think things through.

Whether sharing at home or in a group setting, plan to begin at a time when you and your child or group are relaxed and have an uninterrupted moment to share an activity. It is important that the adult leading the activity is emotionally available when sitting to do this. This can be hard when you feel rushed and stressed, so choose the timing carefully.

Only you will know how much time and energy you and your child or group are able to give to this practice in each session, and what will suit your setting – dip in; read it completely; return to it again at times in the future. No matter what, **don't push things** – try out the bits that your child or group are most drawn to. Have a go at different activities when they feel right for the progression of the individual or group. Use each approach at a time and place that is **most helpful**.

The activities are catalysts for conversations about how children feel. Once the creativity starts flowing, the session may well grow beyond what's in these pages. Maybe a child has their own ideas about ways to feel a bit better that they could share with you or the group? Try to **listen** and not offer unwelcome solutions or critiques. It can be hard when you want to help, but trust that **with love, support, and encouragement,** children can usually find their own way through.

Also, take **notice of your own feelings** and responses as your child or group creates, and be mindful that you are modelling how to manage and regulate emotions. You do not need to get it right all the time; **be kind to yourself**, just as we encourage the children to be throughout this book. Helping children is not always easy.

In a group setting it is very important to make sure every child feels safe to share and participate. Establish a rapport of **support** and **zero judgement** of their art and expression of emotion.

But keep in mind that some children may need to have additional, dedicated help beyond what is appropriate to do on your own in a classroom or group setting. See page 32 for quick-reference contacts if you feel your child or group member needs further professional or anonymous assistance.

If you are concerned that a child is struggling to cope, then it is worth seeking advice from a professional.

American Art Therapy Association
arttherapy.org/art-therapist-locator

Learn more about art therapy and find a trained therapist to continue emotional work with a creative approach.

Find a Warmline
www.warmline.org

Warmlines are confidential, free phone services that offer emotional support to people who just need someone to talk to. Find a Warmline near you here.

Kids Help Phone
1-800-668-6868
kidshelpphone.ca

Kids Help Phone is a Canadian e-mental health service for youths with counselors available 24 hours a day.

National Mental Health Hotline
1-866-903-3787
mentalhealthhotline.org

This free, 24-hour help line connects people in need with caring, knowledgeable, licensed mental health counselors.

Nemours Kids Health
kidshealth.org

This website is full of helpful health resources for parents, kids, teens, and educators.